TIM JEFFS ART
—Animal Sketches—
Sharks
Coloring Book

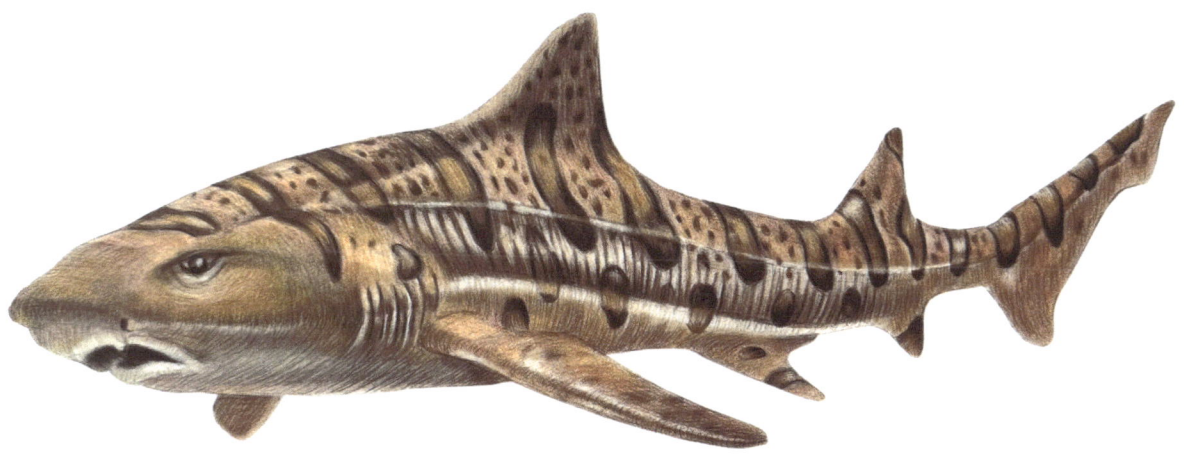

For Jane, Jenna and Harrison

Dedicated to all of the wonderful colorists who have supported my art and made my drawings
more beautiful with their colors, and all the precious creatures that we live among.
A special thank you to Jo Warren for all of her continued support and beautiful colorings
and lesson that make this book so much more special, and Karl Jennings for all of his continued support.

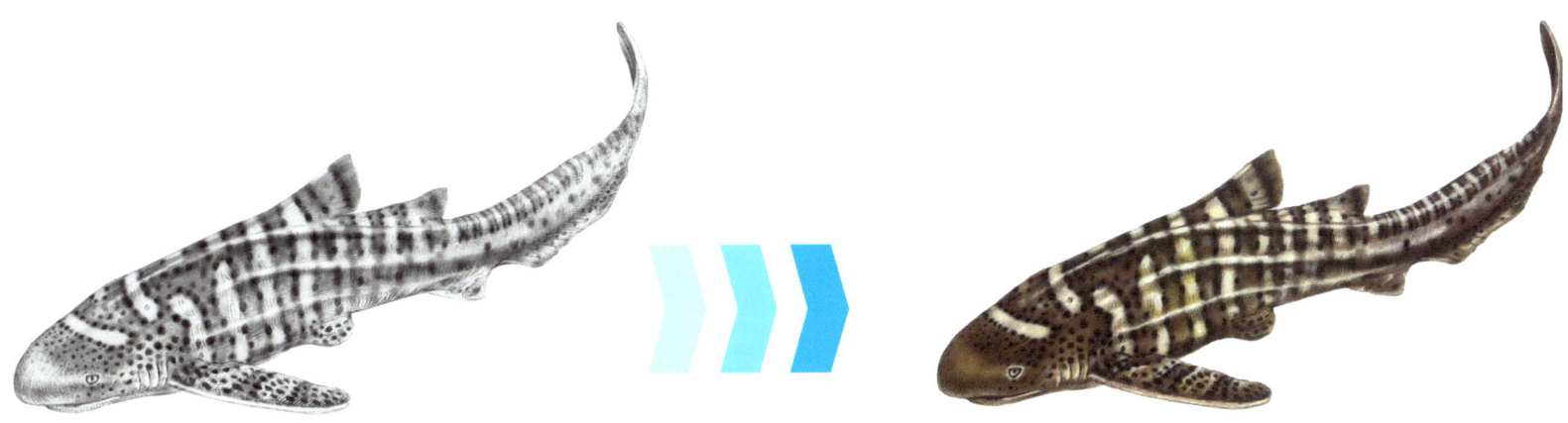

Grayscale coloring page before...

...and after you bring it to life with your colorful imagination!

Tim Jeffs Art
376 East Madison Avenue, Dumont, NJ 07628

Shark Thoughts

Millions of years in the making. Eugenie Clark, an American ichthyologist, who was known as the Shark Lady once said "Sharks are among the most perfectly constructed creatures in nature. Some forms have survived for 200 million years". These remarkable apex predators have kept our oceans in balance, but recently have become threatened by human stigma's, climate change, and overfishing.

I have always had a deep fascination and love for sharks and drawing them. Taking up scuba diving as a teenager I was fortunate enough to enter their ocean world and experience them in nature. From Diving with Sand Tigers off the North Carolina coast, Hammerheads off of the Florida Keys, Mako's in the Bahamas, and White Tips in Micronesia, I learned to respect their strength and understood that the fear of sharks as killers that we are taught isn't necessary.

Shark tooth fossil hunting has become another passion of my family's. We have gone hunting in the fossil beds in rivers of New Jersey, and on the beaches of North Carolina. Finding a shark tooth that's 10's of millions of years old is the ultimate treasure to find, and a wonderful way to learn about shark history.

I hope you enjoy coloring this group of shark sketches as much as I enjoyed drawing them, and I know that with your colors, you will bring them swimming to life!

Great White Shark Coloring Lesson

On the next page I will walk you through the coloring of the Great White Shark which you can find on page 5 of this coloring book. This amazing creature has been swimming the worlds oceans for millions of years and is the largest predatory fish and can live up to 70 years and grow to a length over 20 feet long. Enjoy bringing this extraordinary fish to life with your colorful imagination!

❯ Supply List

In this lesson, Faber Castell Polychromos pencils were used, (pencil numbers listed below) but you can use any brand with similar colors.

1) **The coloring page can be found on page 5**

2) **Colors** (from left to right):

(154) Light Cobalt Turquoise
(101) White
(232) Cold Grey III
(152) Middle Phthalo Blue
(110) Phthalo Blue
(155) Helio Turquoise
(149) Bluish Turquoise

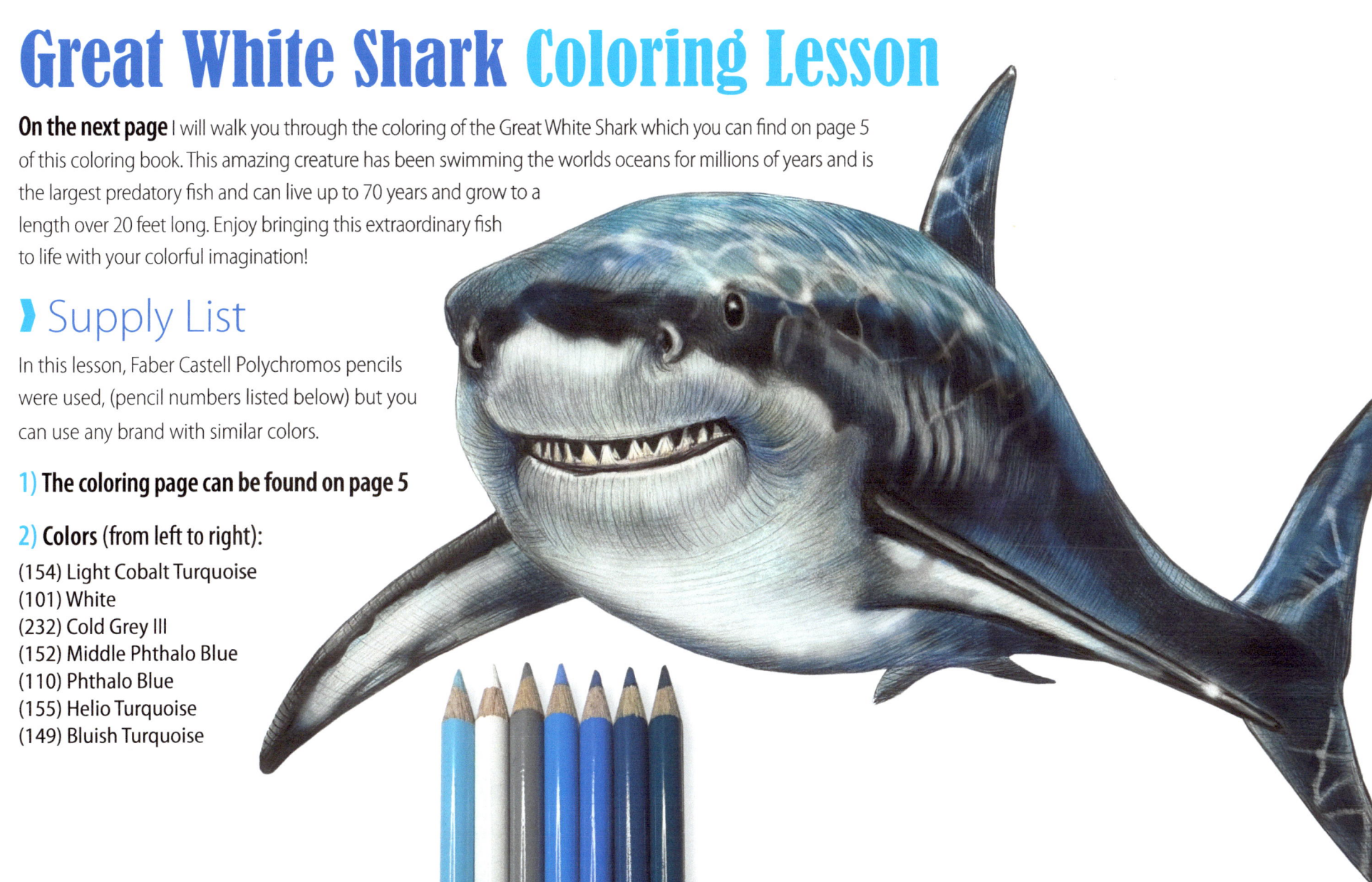

Great White Shark Coloring Lesson

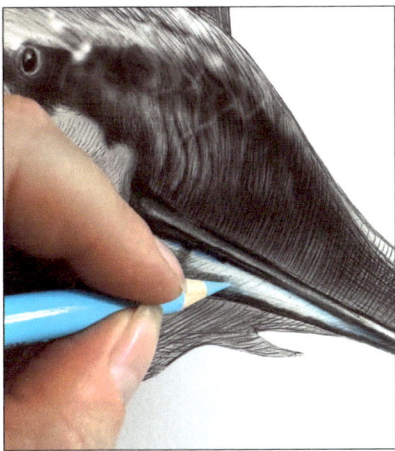

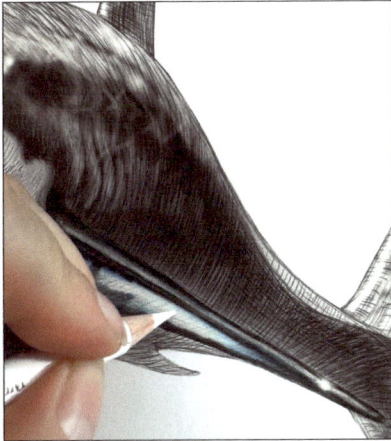

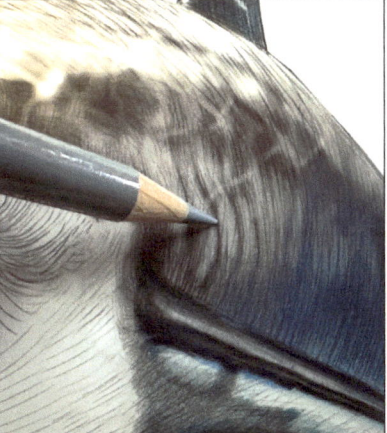

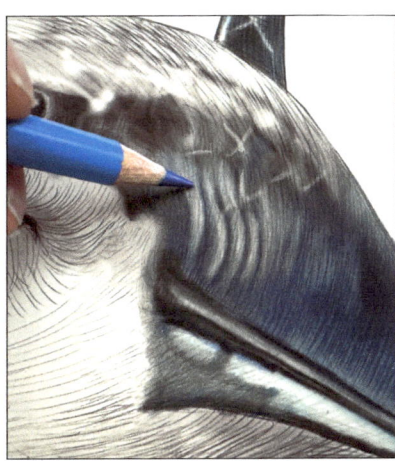

Step 1. Color in the bottom edges of the sharks pectoral fins using Light Cobalt Turquoise (154). Do this several times to build up enough color for the next step which involves blending two colors together.

Step 2. Now take your White (101) colored pencil and fill in the rest of the bottom of the fin, and continue to blend over color (154) in a circular motion to soften the edges between the two colors.

Step 3. Using Cold Grey III (232)color in the side of the Great White Shark. To create shape apply more layers of color directly above the pectoral fins and less color as you move toward the top of the body. Accent the gill slit lines with the same color.

Step 4. Layer color Middle Phthalo Blue (152) over the same section from step 3. This will create even more shape while giving your shark a translucent blue glow as if being underwater. Feel free to use this technique on any of the darker areas of the shark.

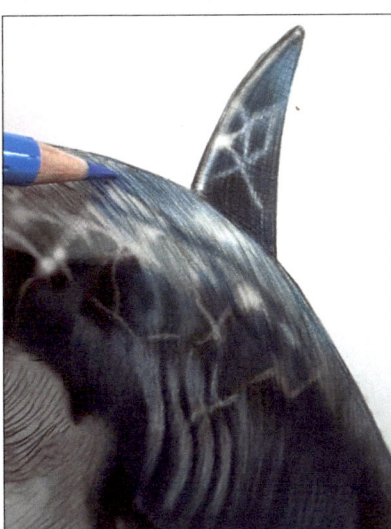

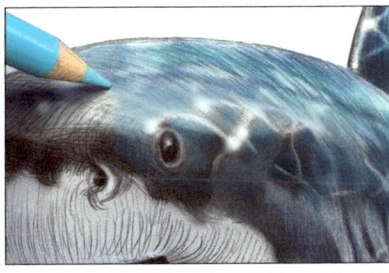

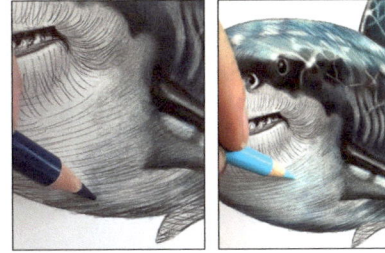

Step 5. Color over the dark areas on the sharks back, dorsal fin and tail fin using Phthalo Blue (110). Try to avoid coloring too much on the light reflective areas, especially the white shiny spots. Leaving these spots white will give the illusion of a bright highlight.

Step 6. Add a layer of light blue to the shark's back using (154). Again avoiding coloring over the bright white highlights. Finally lightly layer and blend Helio Turquois (155) and (154) on the sharks belly to create even more of a rounded 3 dimensional look.

**You did it!
Your Great White
Shark is finished!**

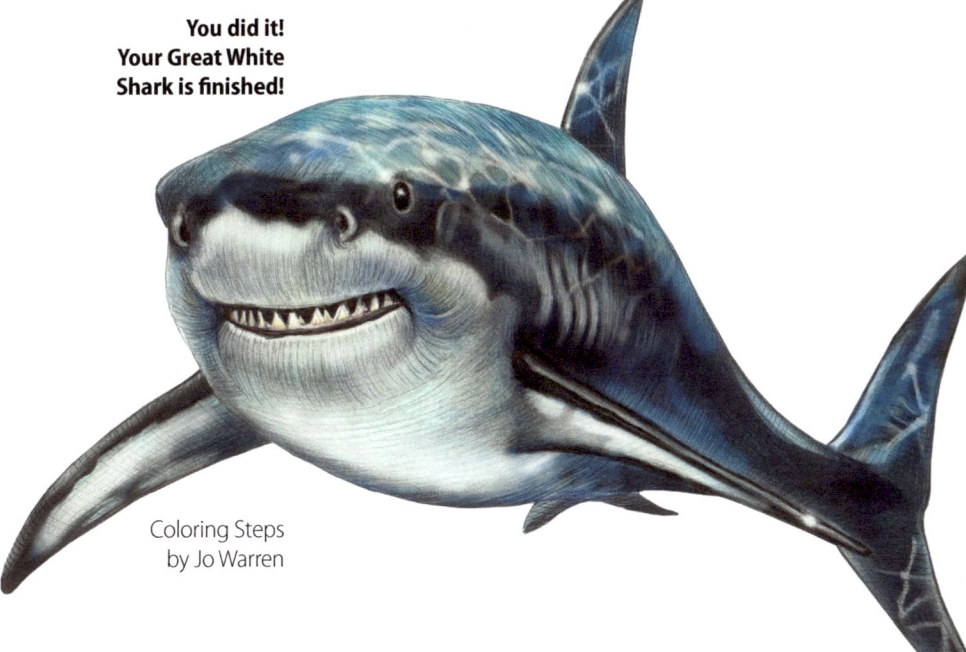

Coloring Steps
by Jo Warren

Spreading Awareness through Coloring

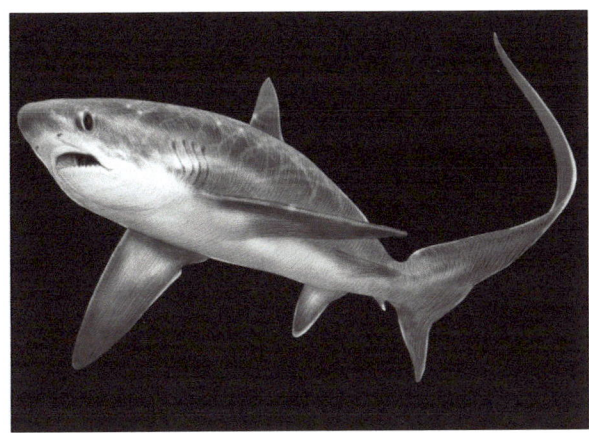

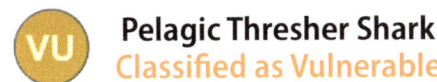

Pelagic Thresher Shark
Classified as Vulnerable

I truly believe that raising awareness through the sharing of my artwork is a fantastic way to educate people about conservation. And coloring animals is a beautiful way to learn about them as you enjoy a relaxing and fun pastime. On the following page, I listed the sharks statuses on the *International Union for Conservation of Nature's (IUCN)* conservation list. I think it's important to include the *(IUCN)* conservation list so people understand the classifications more clearly. To the right is an overview of the IUCN's conservation list, which breaks animals' conservation statuses into several categories. Knowing what these categories mean and the animals that are included in them is extremely important. **Together through art and coloring we can change the world!**

Tim Jeffs
Animal Artist

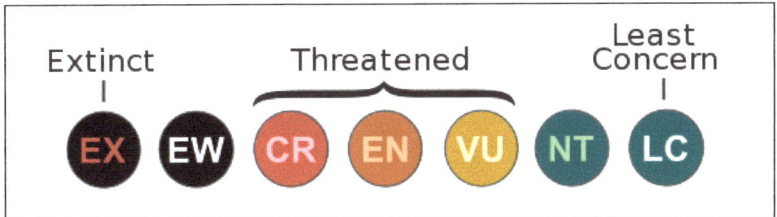

The list consists of 7 categories. From Least Concerned all the way to Extinct. Here are the definitions of each category:

• **LEAST CONCERN (LC):** A species that has been evaluated but not qualified for any other category on the list.

• **NEAR THREATENED (NT):** A species that may be considered threatened with extinction in the near future.

• **VULNERABLE (VU):** A species likely to become endangered unless the circumstances that are threatening its survival and reproduction improve.

• **ENDANGERED (EN):** A species that is considered very likely to become extinct.

• **CRITICALLY ENDANGERED (CR):** A species that is facing an extremely high risk of becoming extinct in the wild.

• **EXTINCT IN THE WILD (EW):** A species that is only known by living members kept in captivity or as a naturalized population outside its historic range due to massive habitat loss.

• **EXTINCT (EX):** A species that has been terminated.

Learn about the Sharks

Before you start coloring, it's important to learn about the sharks in this coloring book.

❱ Basking Shark This second-largest living shark reaches 12m and 8 tons. It lives in temperate oceans, filter-feeding on zooplankton. Vulnerable due to overfishing, it's known for its slow movement and large mouth.
Conservation Status: Vulnerable

❱ Blue Shark The sleek Blue Shark grows to 3.8m and 205kg. It thrives globally in temperate seas, primarily feeding on squids and fish. It's near threatened due to commercial fishing.
Conservation Status: Near Threatened

❱ Bull Shark Known for its aggression, the Bull Shark reaches 3.5m and 315kg. It's unique for inhabiting both seawater and freshwater, feeding omnivorously. Overfishing has made it a near-threatened species. **Conservation Status:** Near Threatened

❱ Great Hammerhead Shark Reaching 6m and 580kg, this shark with a unique hammer-like head resides in tropical and warm temperate seas. It feeds on fish, squid, and crustaceans, and is endangered due to overfishing.
Conservation Status: Endangered

❱ Great White Shark Reaching 6.4m and 2 tons, this iconic shark lives globally in coastal areas, feeding on seals, fish, and birds. Overfishing has made it a vulnerable species.
Conservation Status: Vulnerable

❱ Greenland Shark This Arctic and North Atlantic inhabitant is one of the longest living vertebrates with a life expectancy of at least 272 years. Reaching 7.3m and 1 ton. It feeds on fish and seals and is near threatened due to by-catch. **Conservation Status:** Near Threatened

❱ Leopard Shark This small, distinctive shark reaches 1.5m and 18.4kg. It thrives off the Pacific coast, feeding on crustaceans and fish. Though its status is least concern, it faces localized threats.
Conservation Status: Least Concerned

❱ Oceanic Whitetip Shark Known for its distinct white-tipped fins, this shark reaches 4m and 167kg. It inhabits tropical oceans and feeds on squid and fish. Overfishing has critically endangered this species.
Conservation Status: Critically Endangered

❱ Pelagic Thresher Shark The unique Pelagic Thresher, growing to 3.5m and 70kg, is known for its long tail. It lives in tropical and subtropical oceans, feeding on small fish and squids. Overfishing has made it a vulnerable species.
Conservation Status: Vulnerable

❱ Port Jackson Shark Known for its distinctive harness-like markings, this shark reaches 1.65m and 33kg. It resides in Australian waters, feeding on sea urchins and molluscs. Though least concern, it faces localized threats.
Conservation Status: Least Concerned

❱ Sand Tiger Shark This large, slow-moving shark reaches 3.2m and 159kg. It inhabits global coastal areas, feeding on fish and squid. Overfishing has made it a vulnerable species.
Conservation Status: Vulnerable

❱ Shortfin Mako Shark Known for its speed, the Mako grows to 4m and 570kg. It lives in worldwide oceans, feeding on fish and squid. Overfishing has made this an endangered species.
Conservation Status: Endangered

❱ Tiger Shark This large shark with distinctive tiger-like stripes reaches 5.5m and 635kg. It's found in tropical and subtropical oceans, feeding on a wide-ranging diet. It's near threatened due to overfishing. **Conservation Status:** Near Threatened

❱ Whale Shark The largest living fish species, it reaches 18.8m and 34 tons. This gentle giant inhabits tropical oceans and filter-feeds on plankton. It's endangered due to fishing and vessel strikes. **Conservation Status:** Endangered

❱ Zebra Shark Known for its distinctive pattern, this shark reaches 2.5m and 30kg. It inhabits the Indo-Pacific, feeding on molluscs and crustaceans. Despite its relatively docile nature, overfishing and habitat loss have made it an endangered species. **Conservation Status:** Endangered

Sharks on Black Backgrounds Index

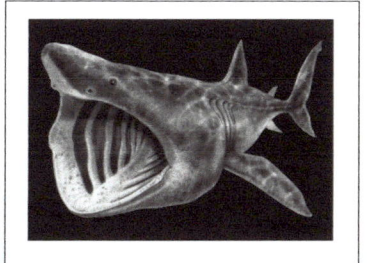

Basking Shark 1

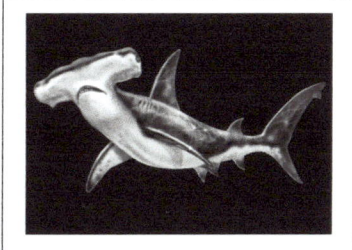

Great Hammerhead Shark 4

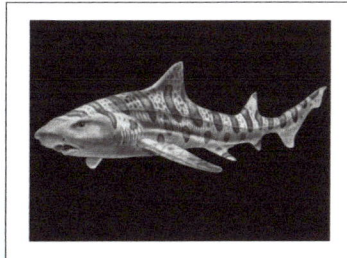

Leopard Shark 7

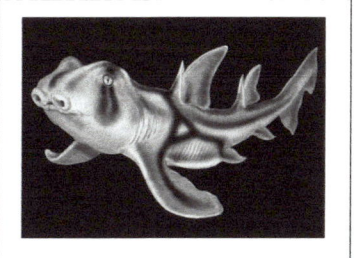

Port Jackson Shark 10

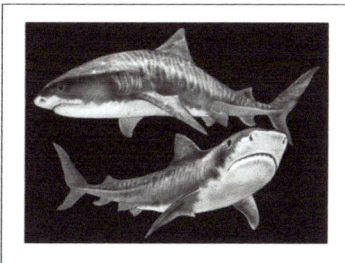

Tiger Sharks 13

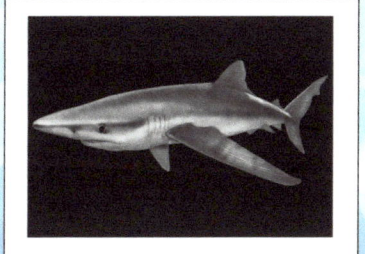

Blue Shark 2

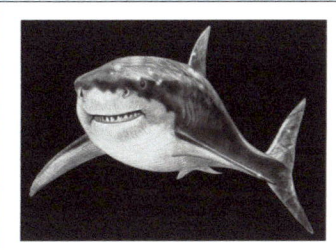

Great White Shark 5

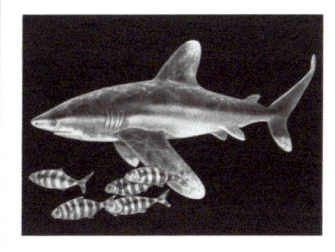

Oceanic Whitetip Shark 8

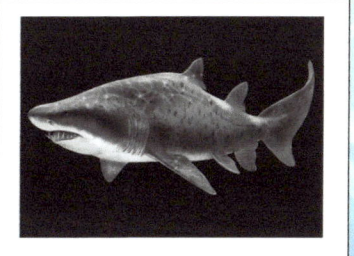

Sand Tiger Shark 11

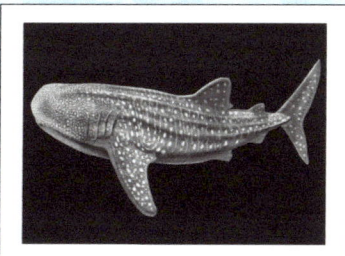

Whale Shark 14

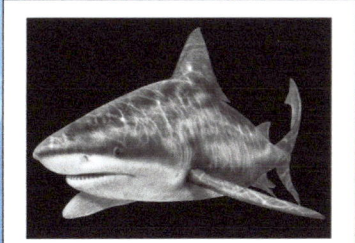

Bull Shark 3

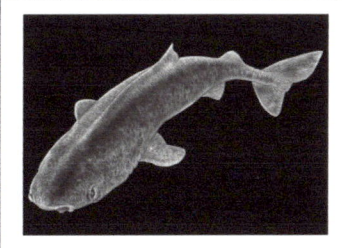

Greenland Shark 6

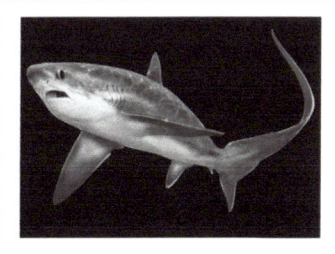

Pelagic Thresher Shark 9

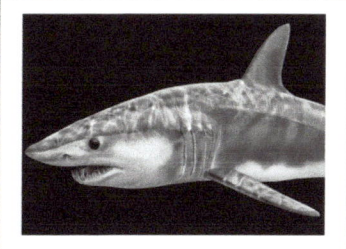

Shortfin Mako Shark 12

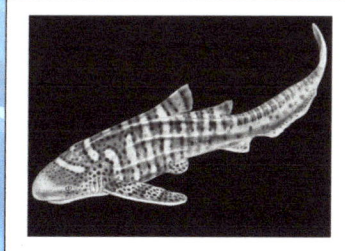

Zebra Shark 15

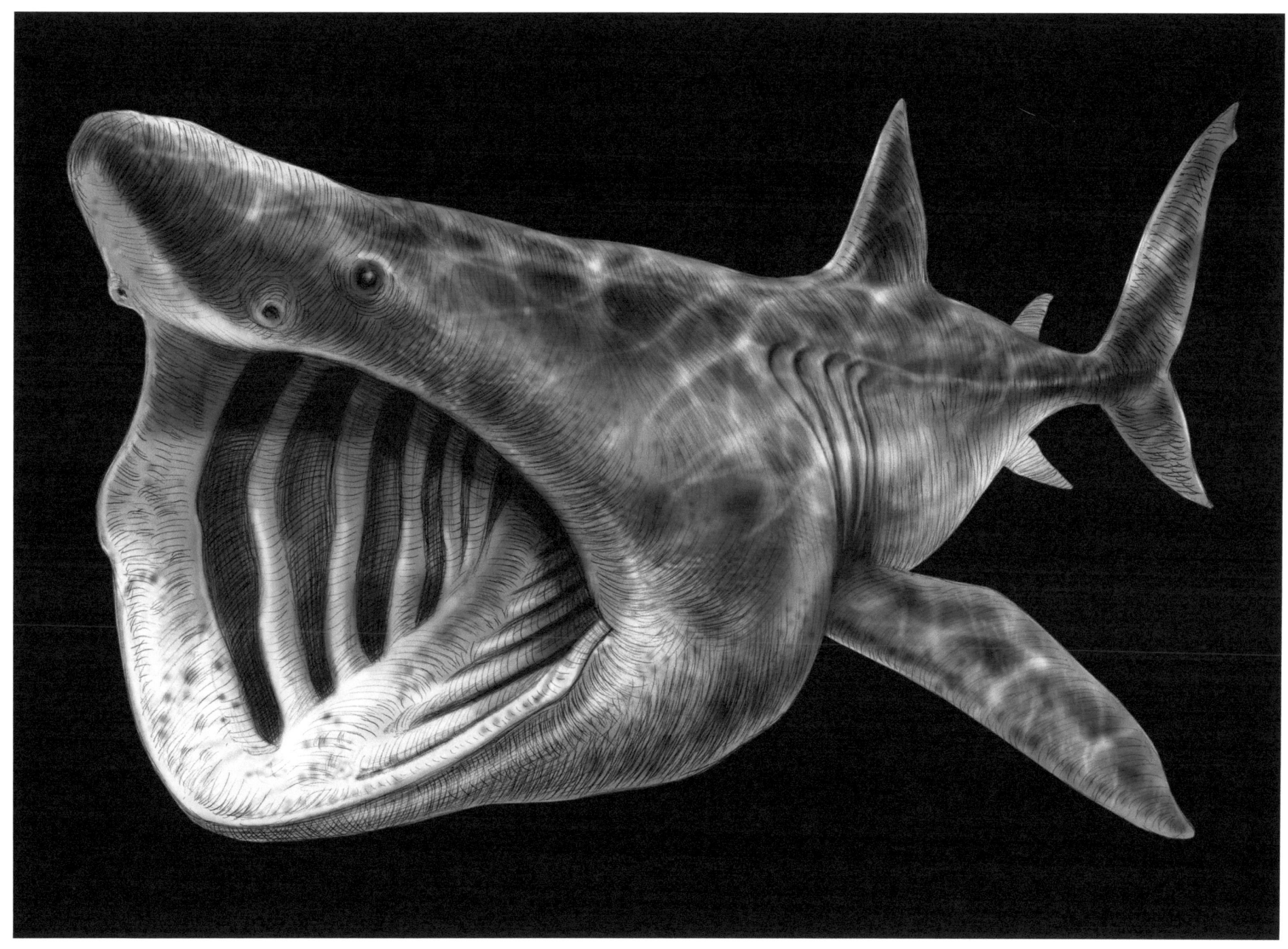

Basking Shark

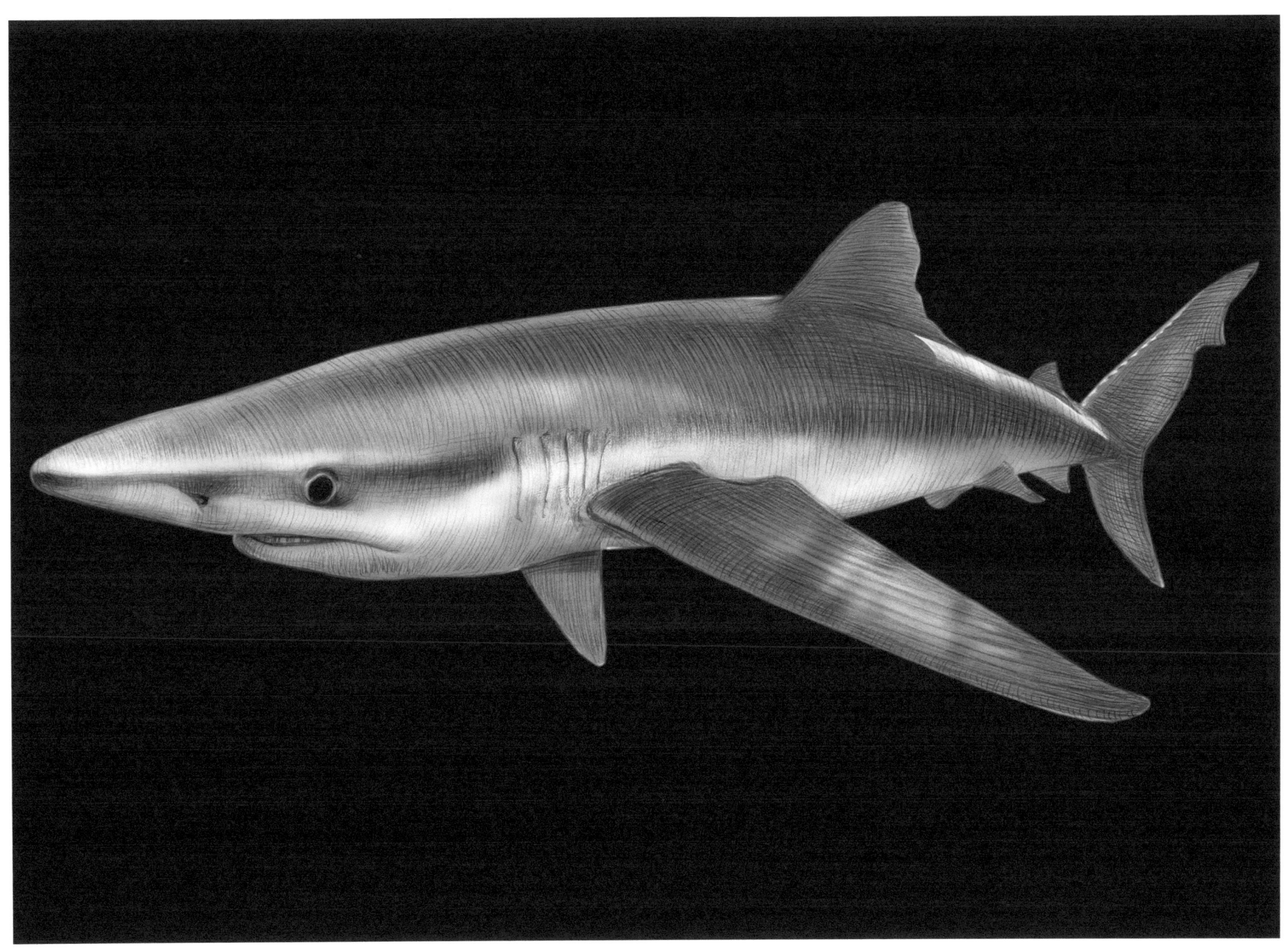

Blue Shark

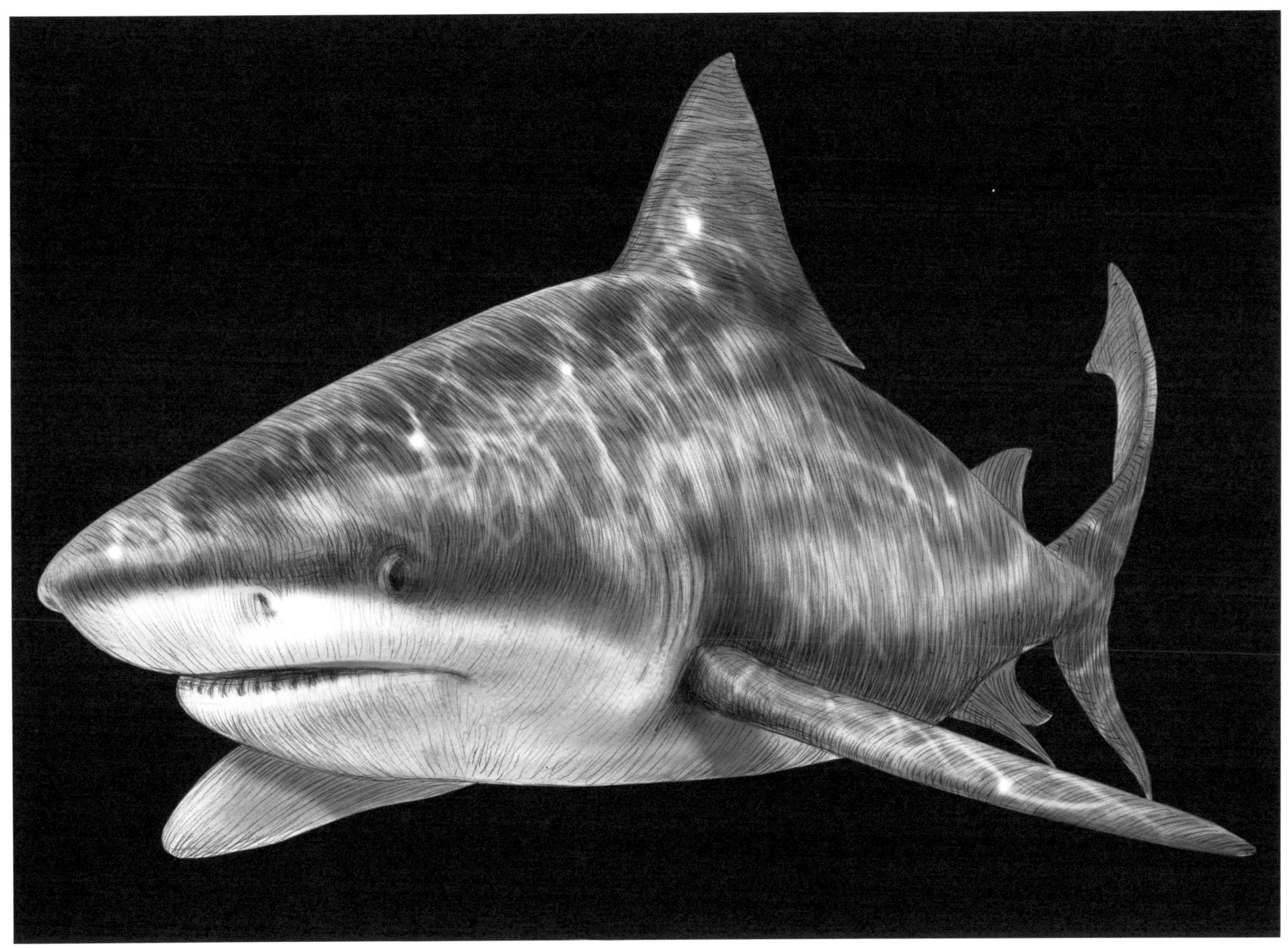

Bull Shark

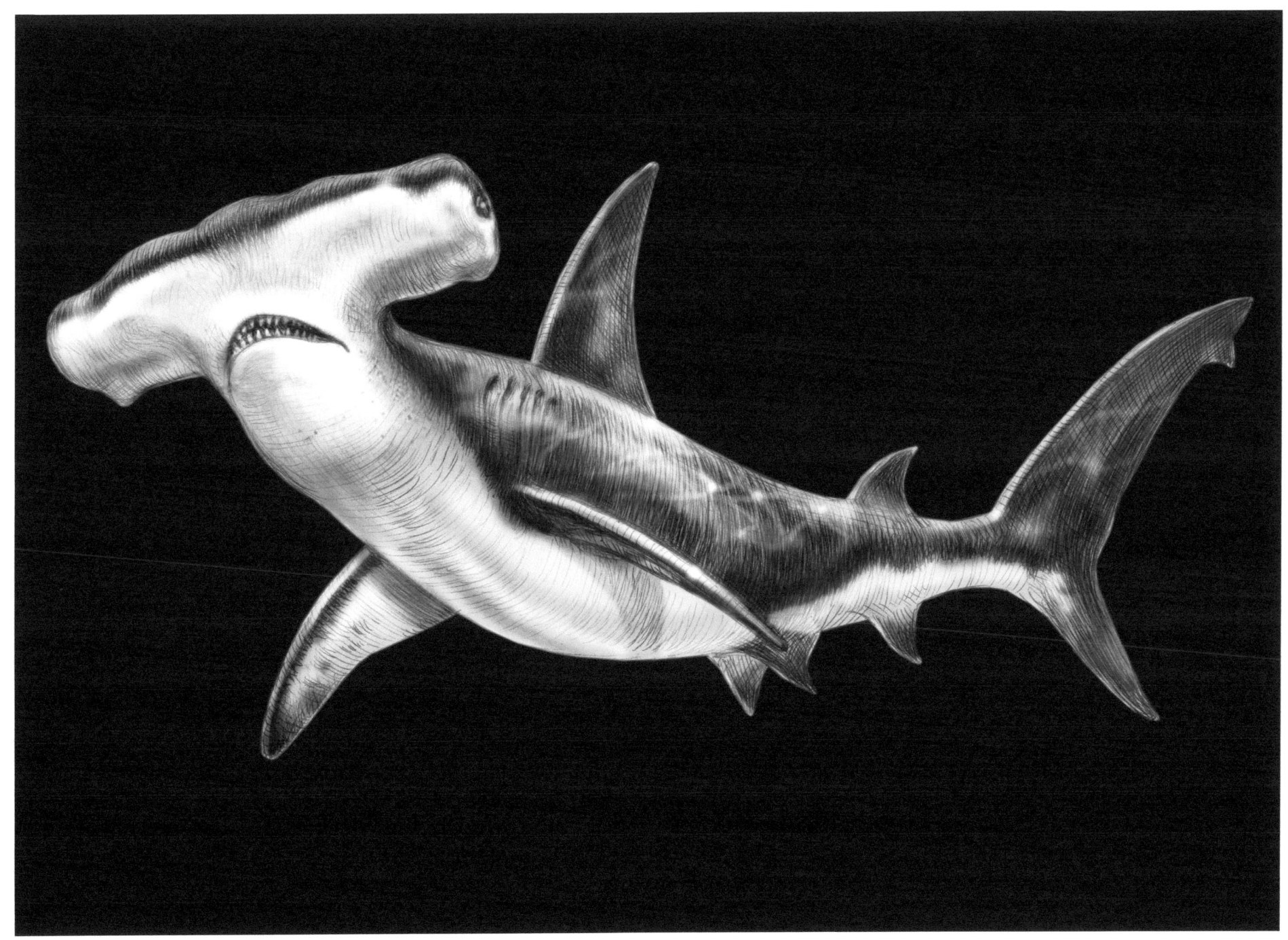

Great Hammerhead Shark

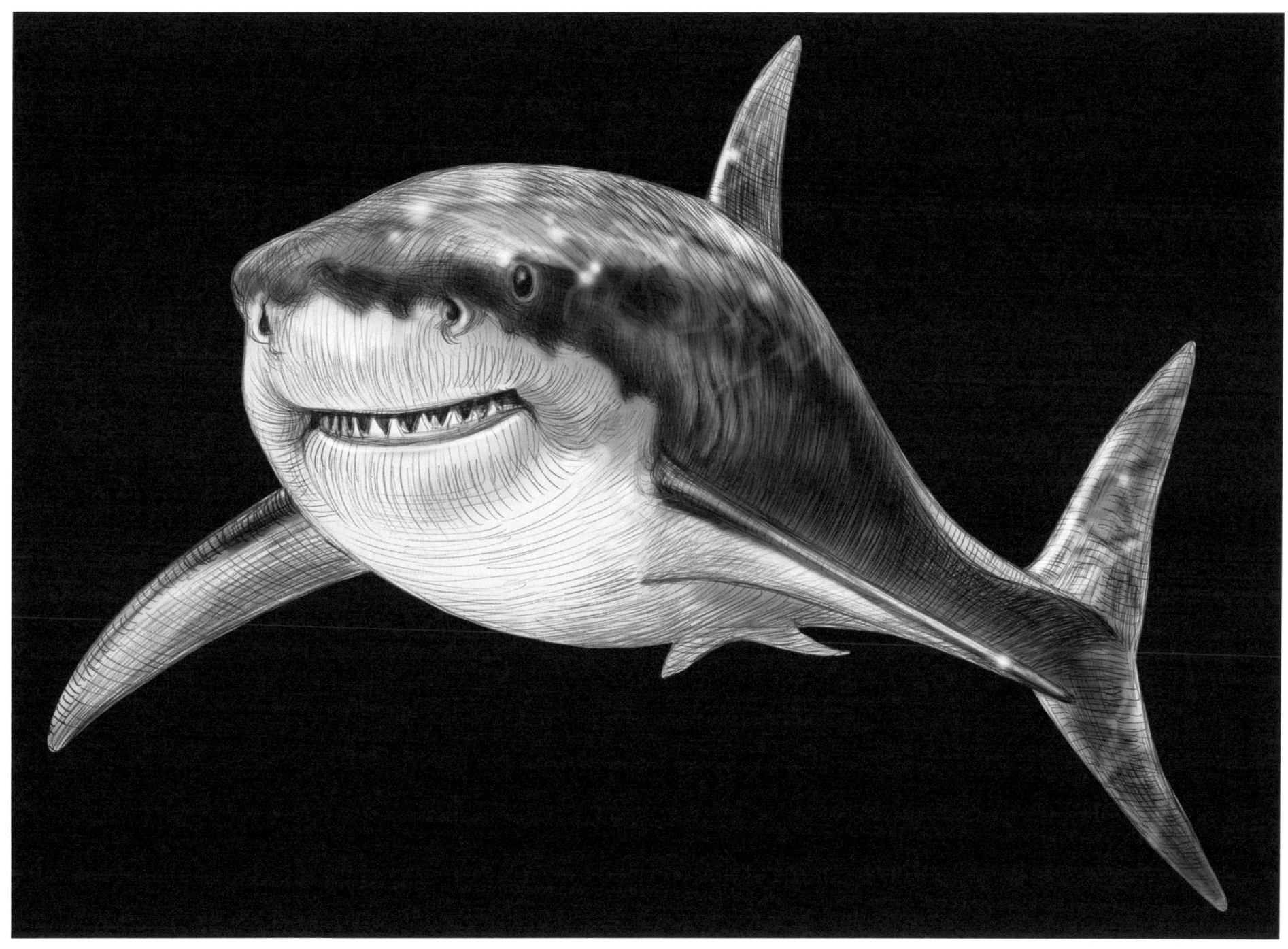

Great White Shark

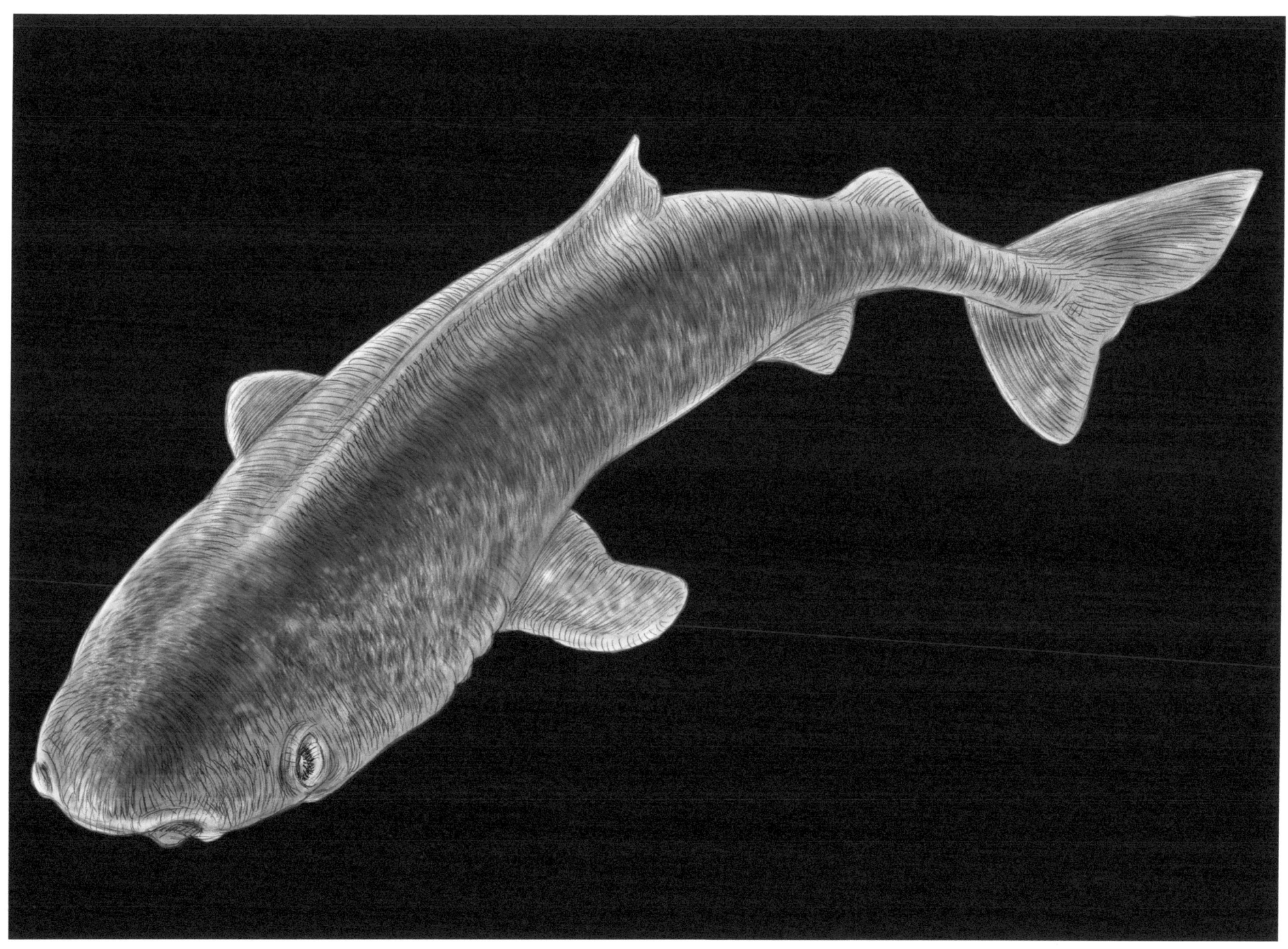

Greenland Shark

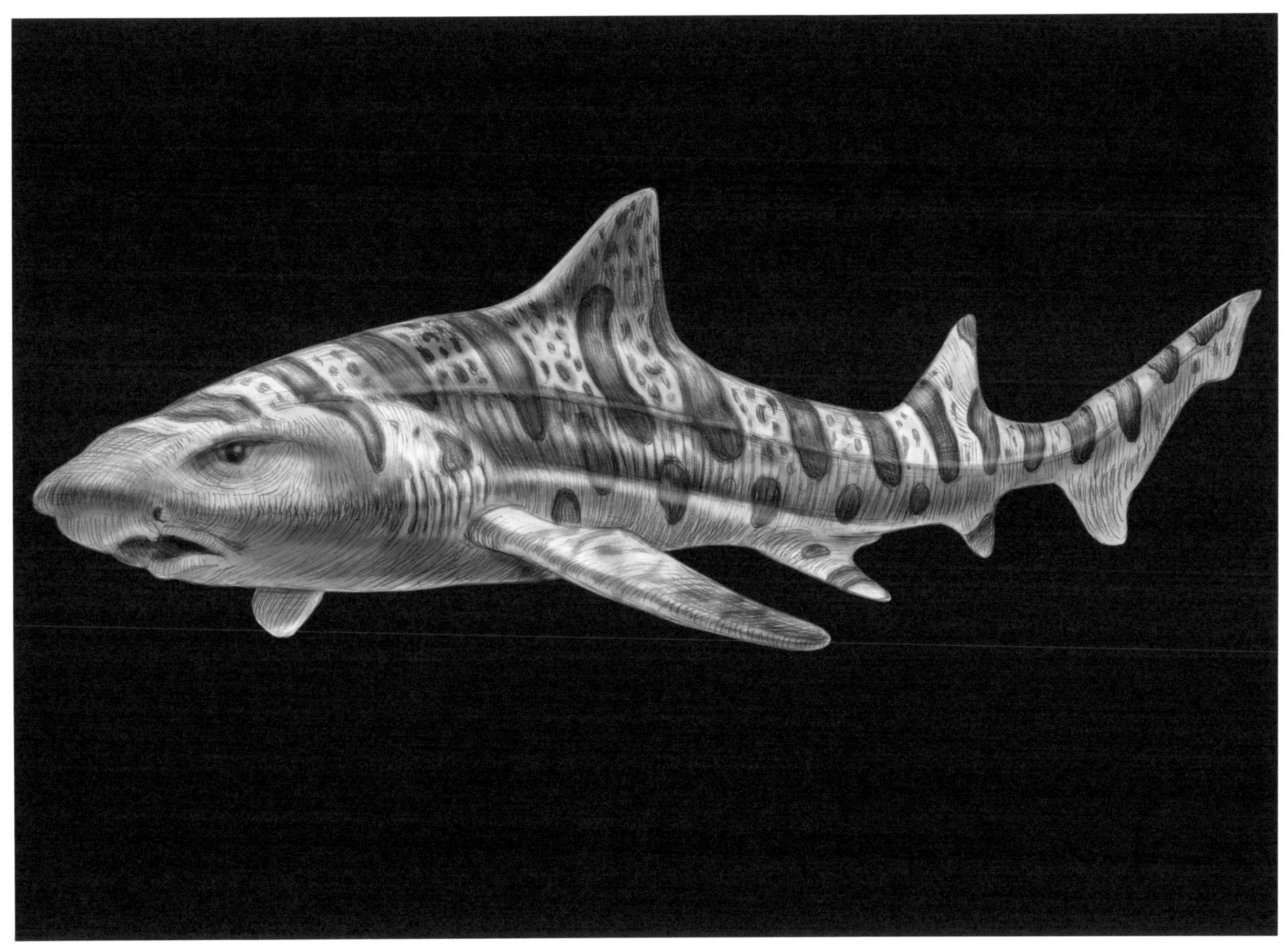

Leopard Shark

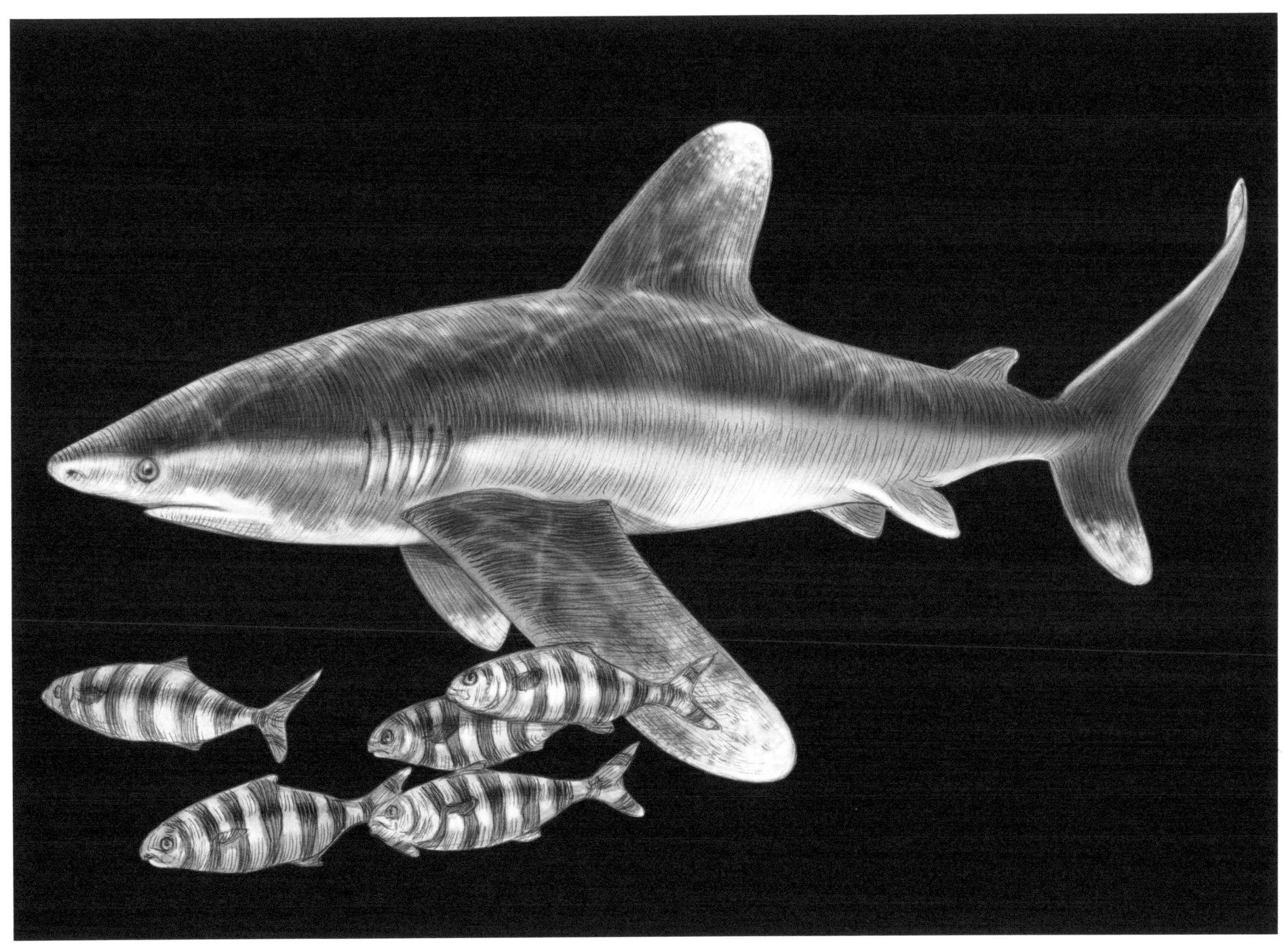

Oceanic Whitetip Shark

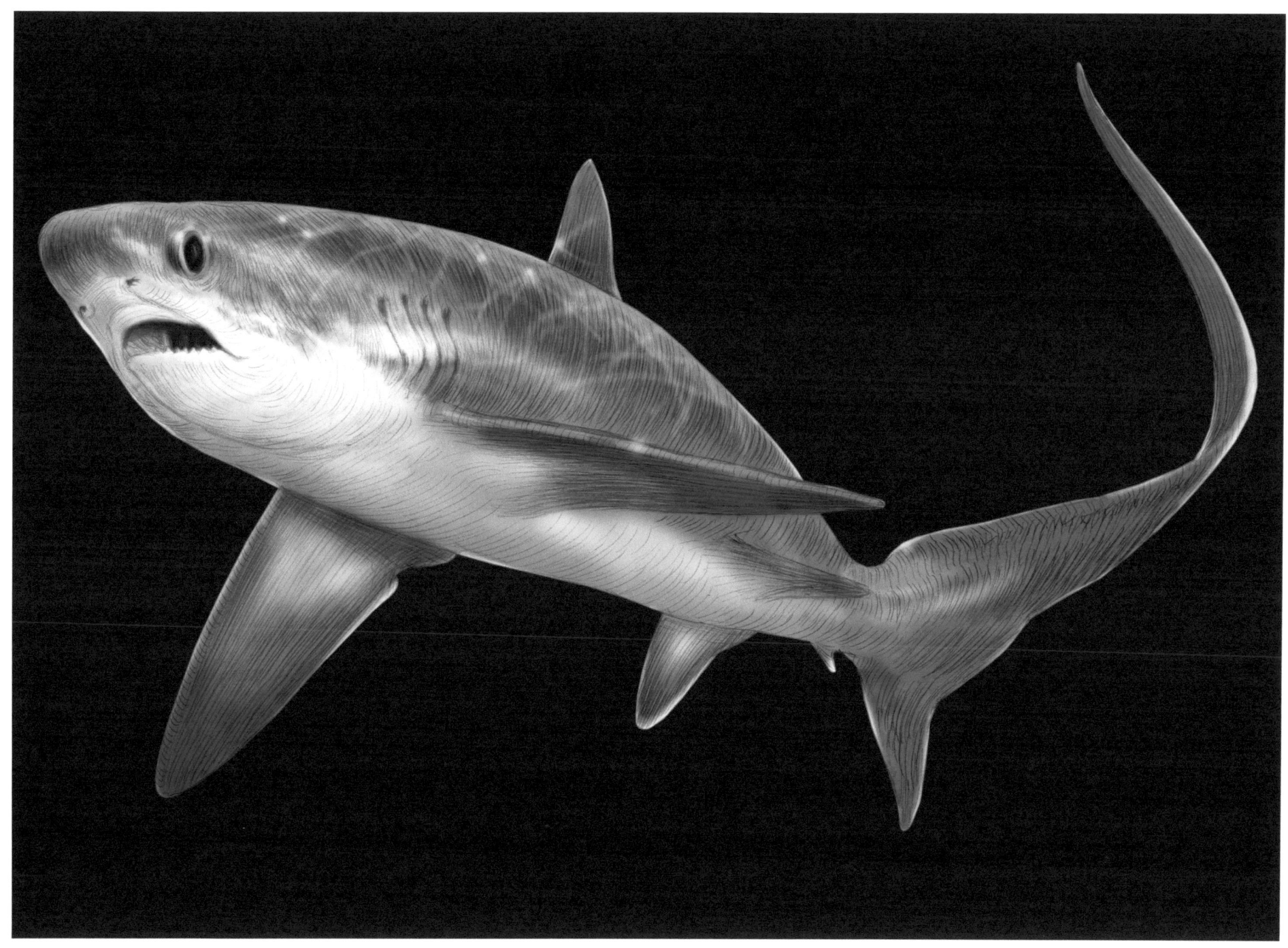

Pelagic Thresher Shark

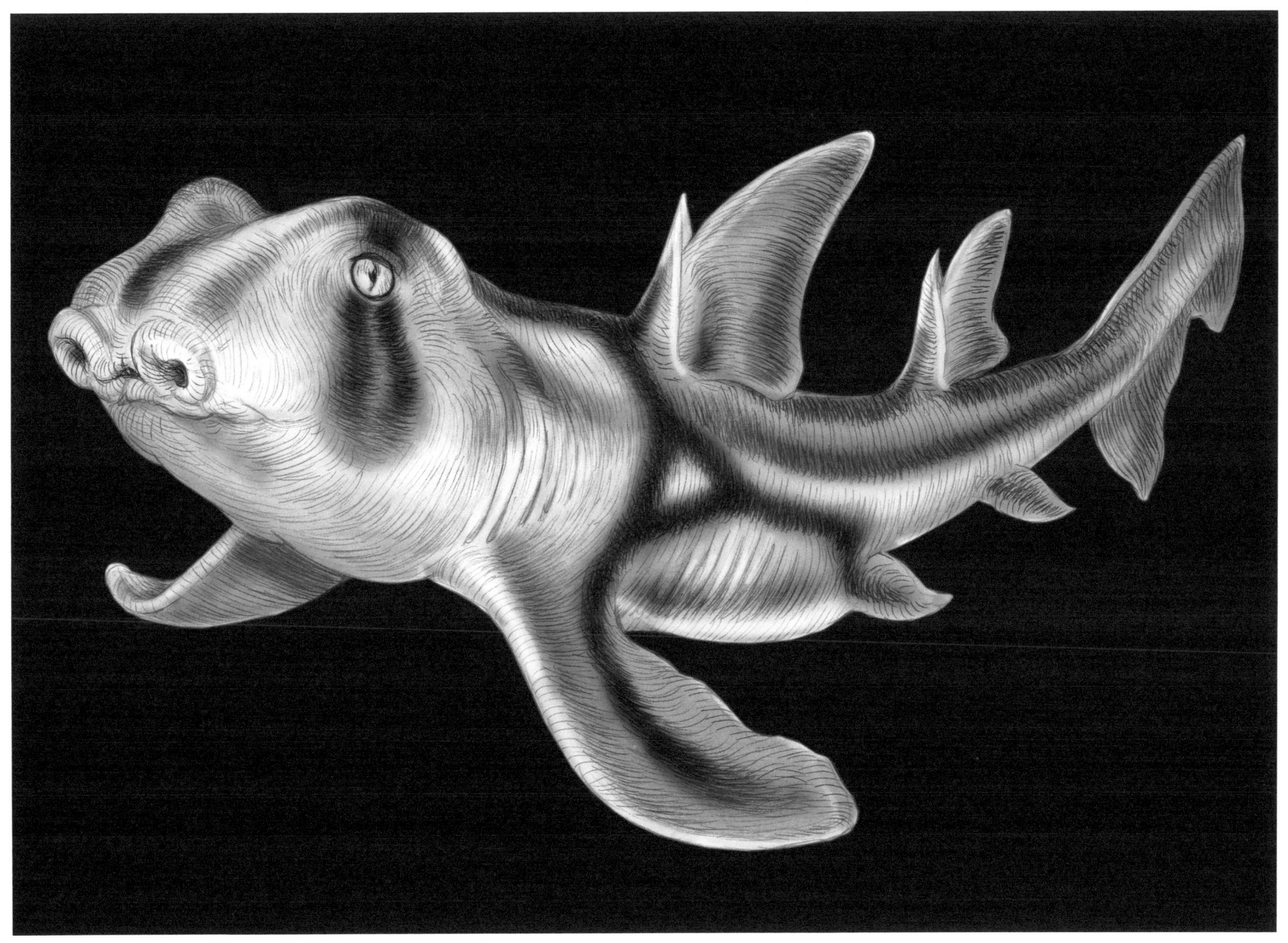

Port Jackson Shark

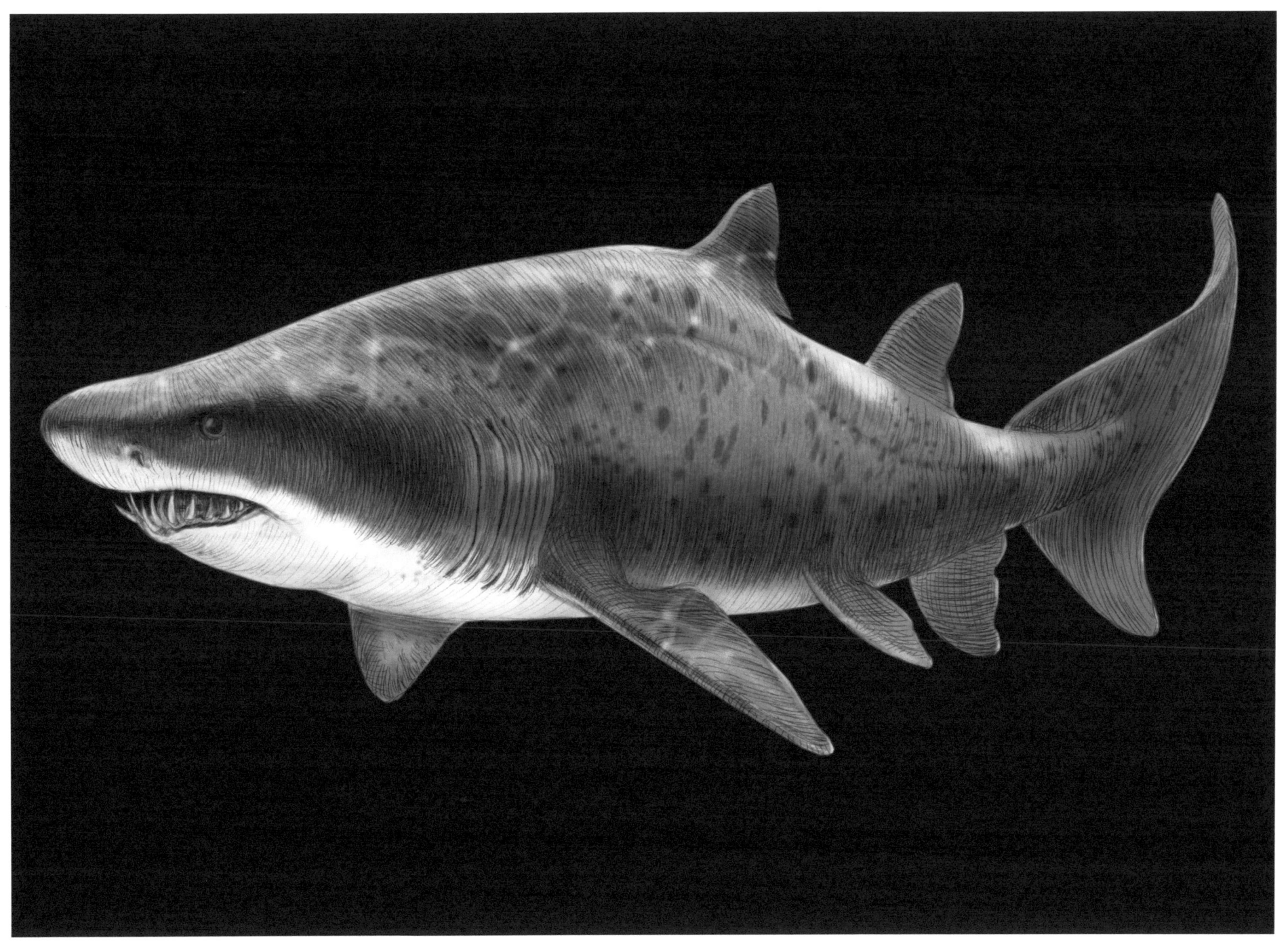

Sand Tiger Shark

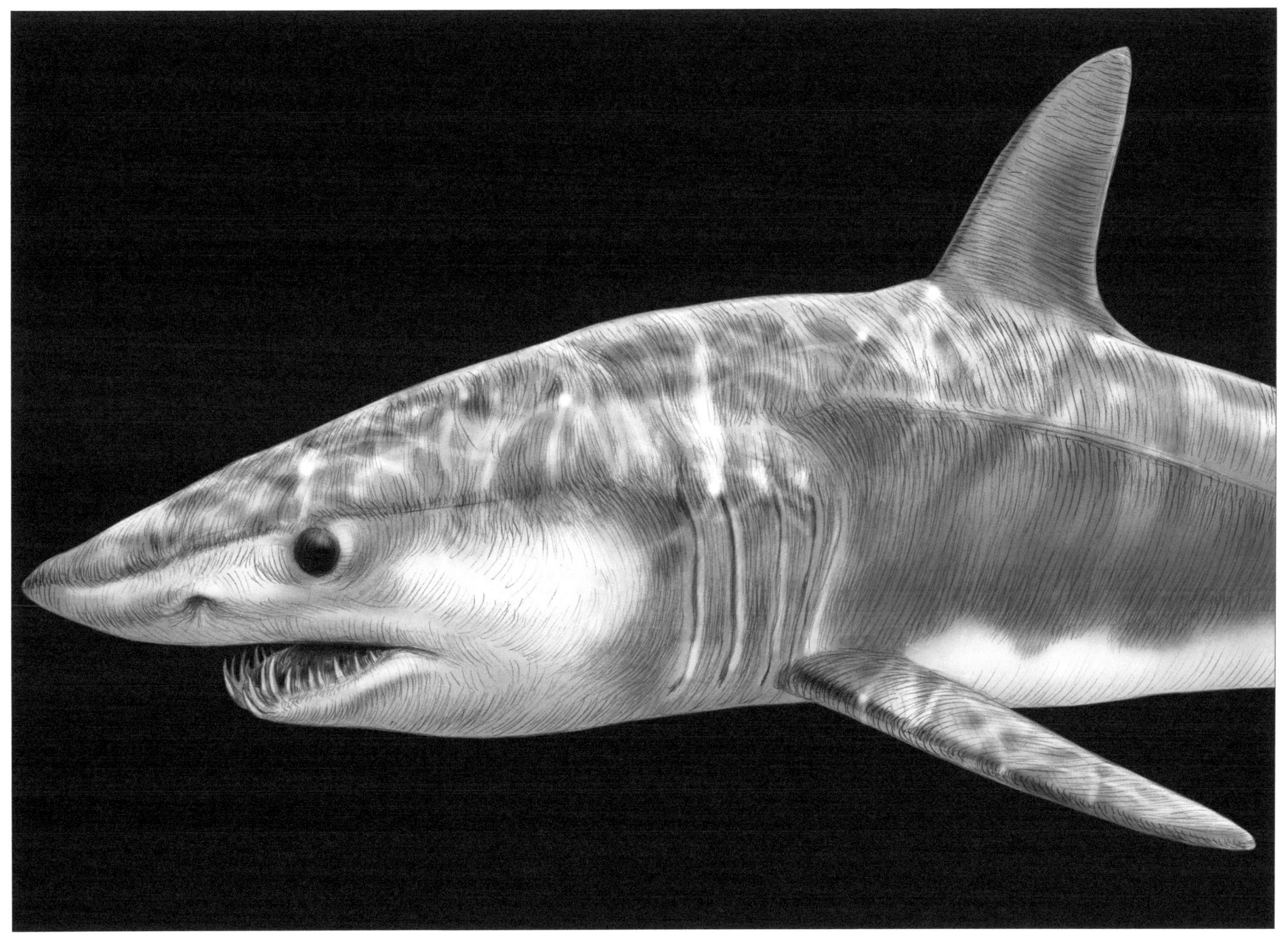

Shortfin Mako Shark

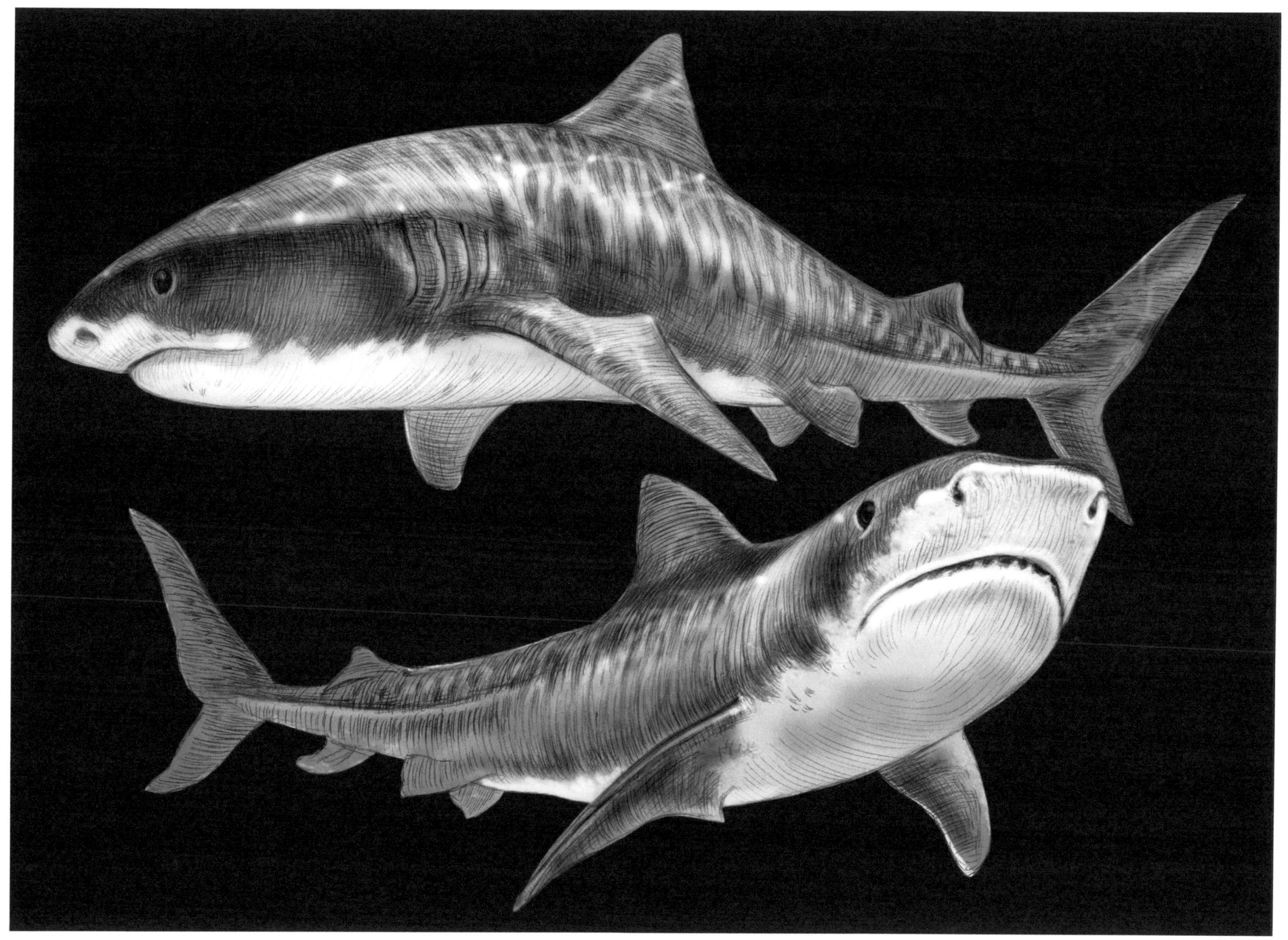

Tiger Sharks

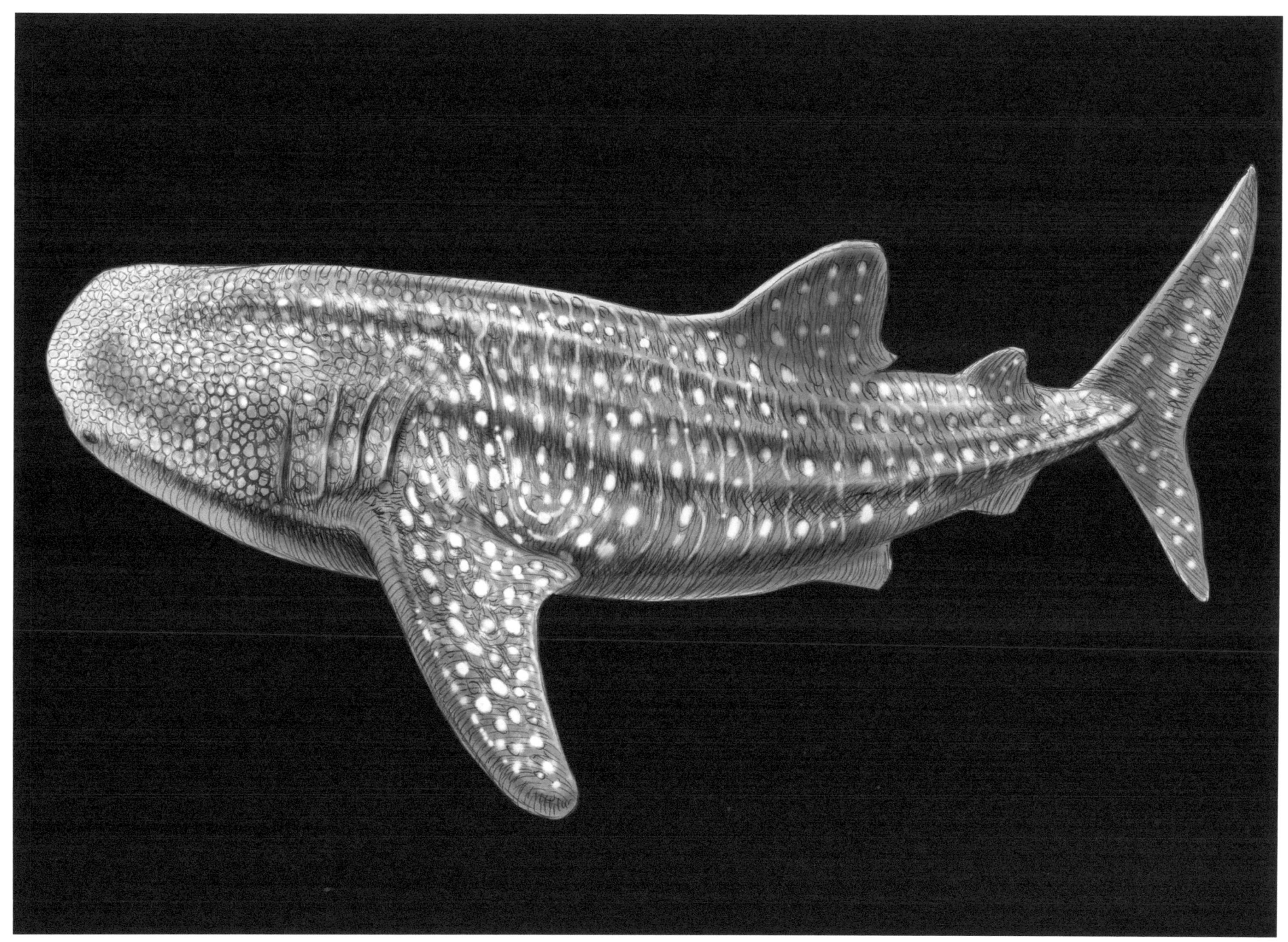

Whale Shark

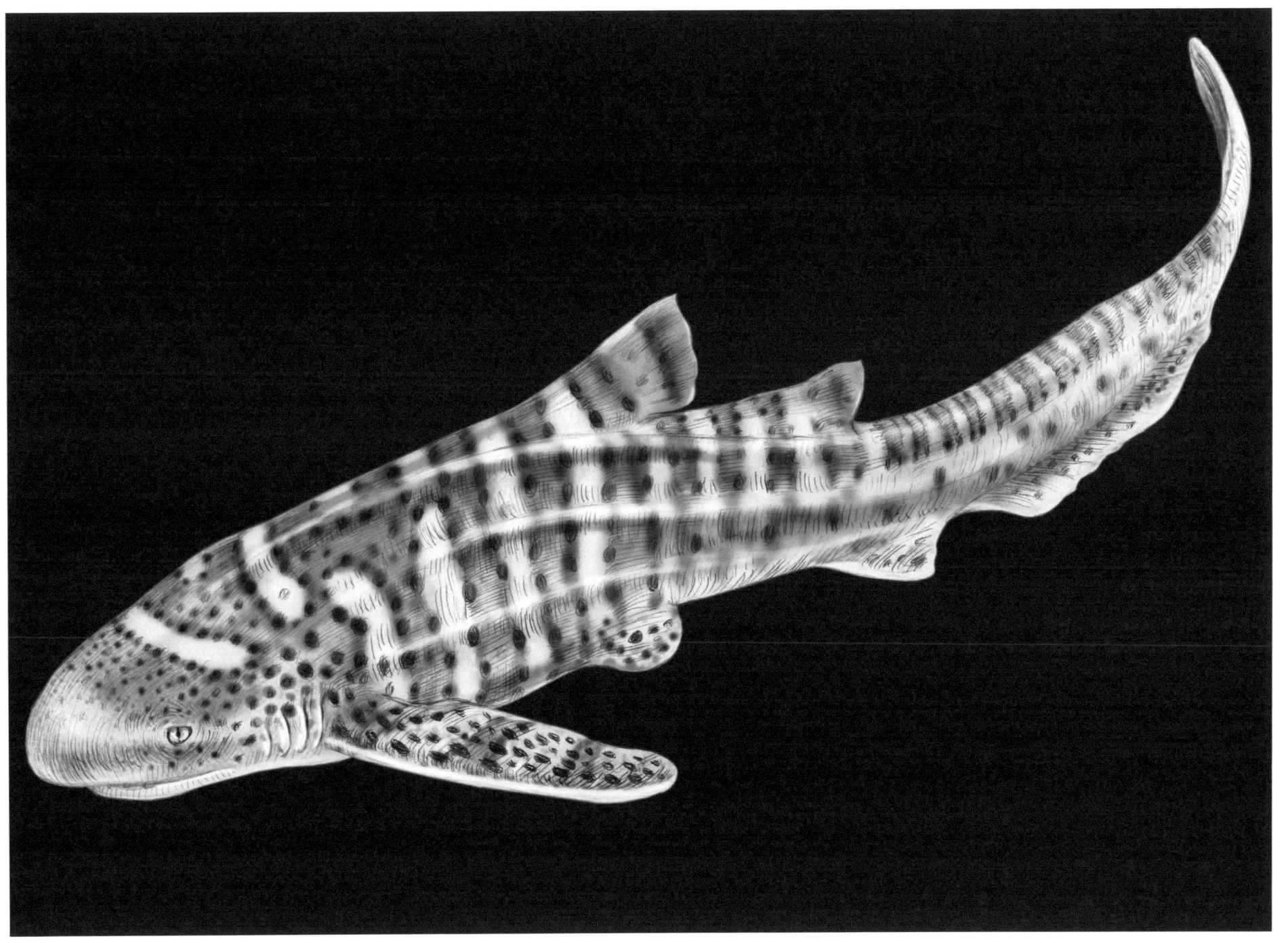

Zebra Shark

Tim Jeffs is a New York City based artist and illustrator who has been creating dynamic artwork for over 25 years. Animals are a favorite subject matter of his, along with the complex and intricate details these creatures possess. *"The incredible diversity and complexity of animals has always intrigued me. They offer endless pleasure to look and marvel upon. In every drawing I try to capture the unique quality of each particular animal. I hope you enjoy my perspective, love and admiration of these incredible creatures."*

Visit my website for prints, digital coloring books and coloring lessons:

www.TimJeffsArt.com

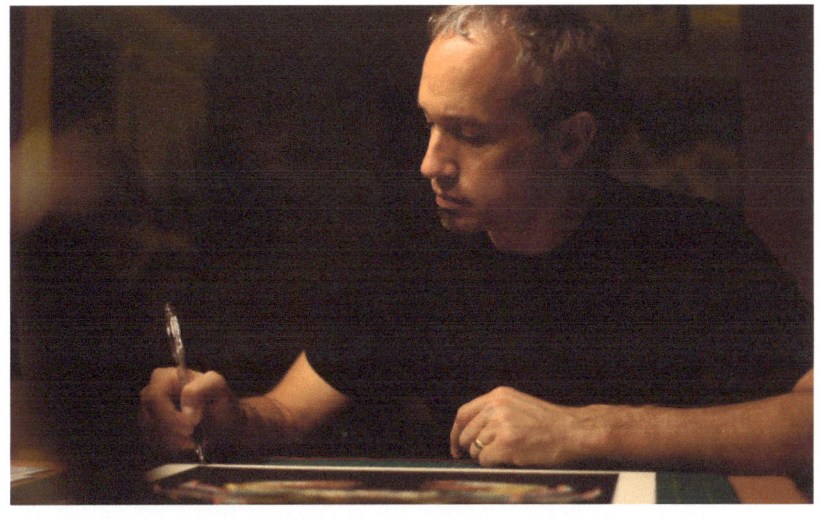

Discover the full line of Tim Jeffs' Published Coloring Books

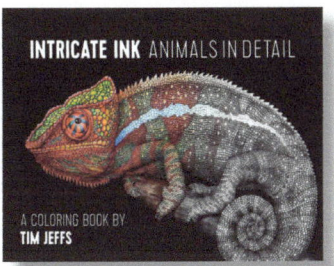
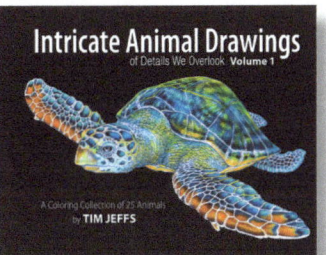
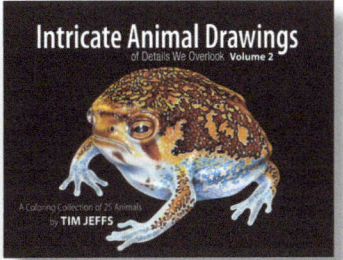
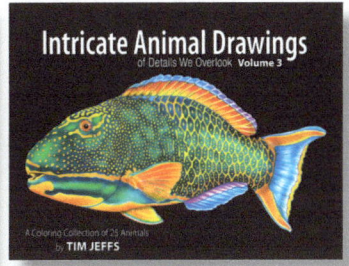
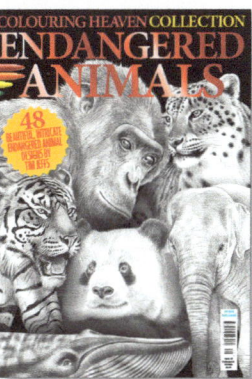

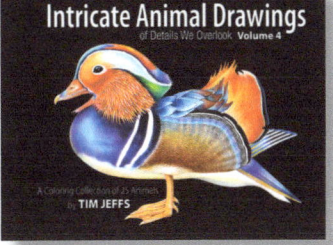
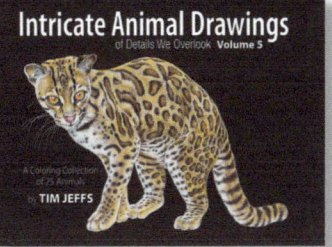

Intricate Ink Animals In Detail Volume 1, and Intricate Animal Drawings Volume 1 through 5 are available at: Amazon.com

Colouring Heaven Collection Endangered Animals
Available at: Colouringheaven.com

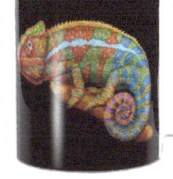

Discover Tim Jeffs' Merchandise

Etsy Shop
www.etsy.com/shop/TimJeffsArt

Society6 Shop
www.society6.com/TimJeffsArt

Redbubble Shop
TimJeffsArt.redbubble.com

TeePublic Shop
https://www.teepublic.com/user/tim-jeffs-art

Discover the full line of Tim Jeffs Coloring Books and Lessons

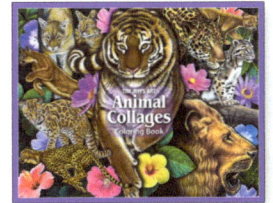 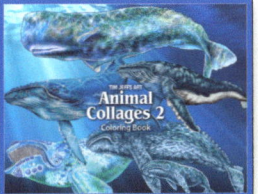 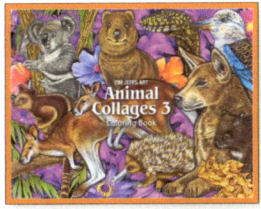 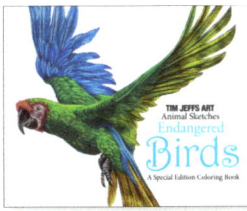 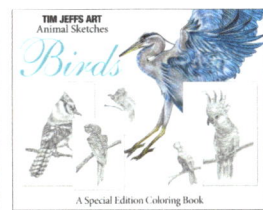 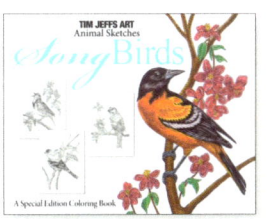 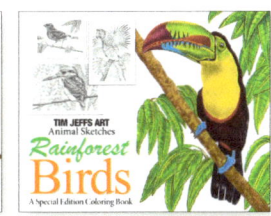

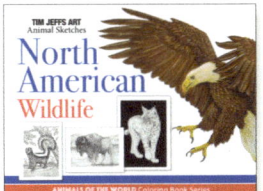 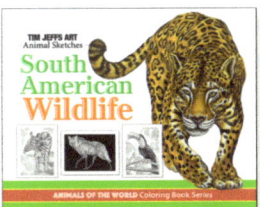 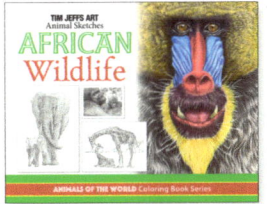 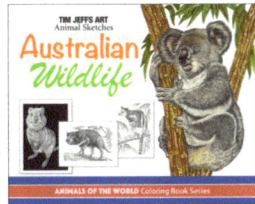 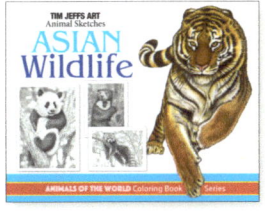 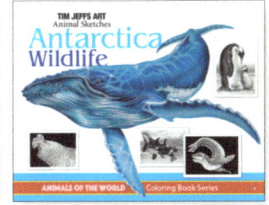 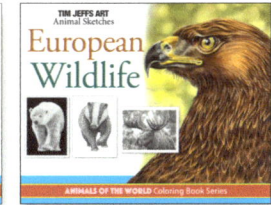

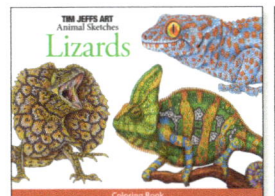 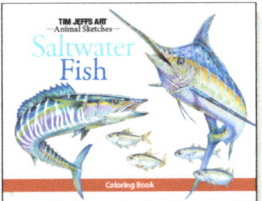 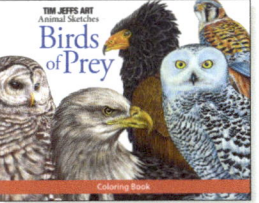 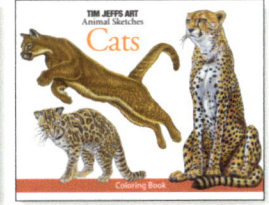 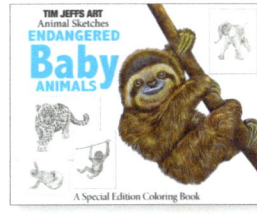 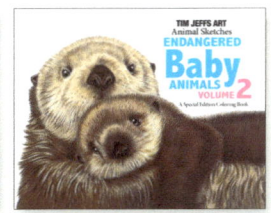 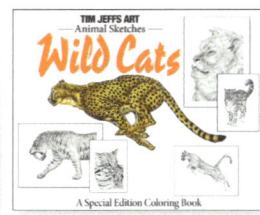

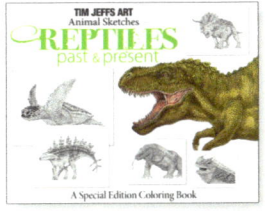 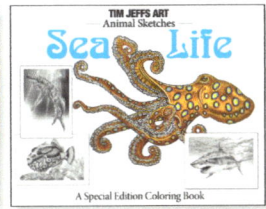 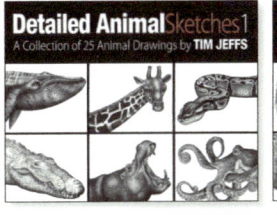 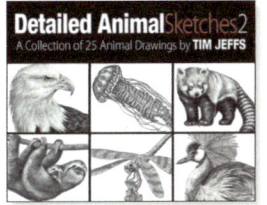 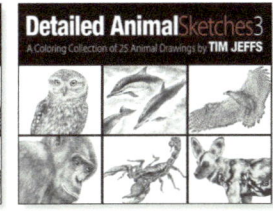 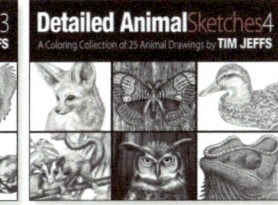 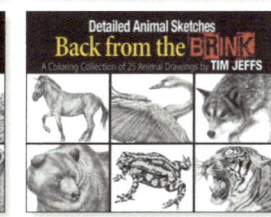

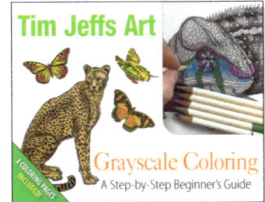 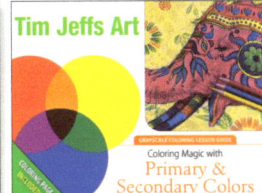 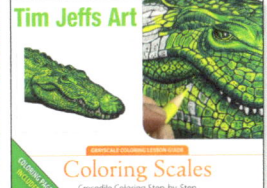 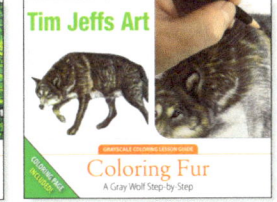 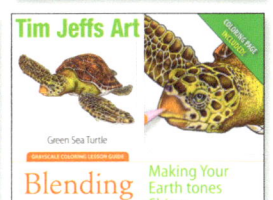 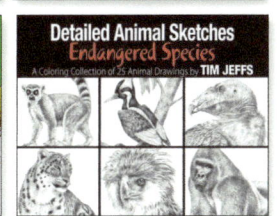 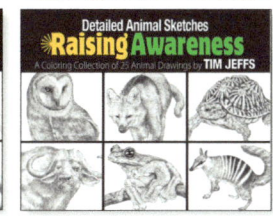

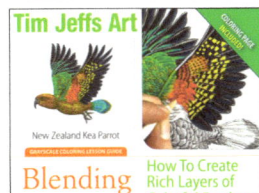 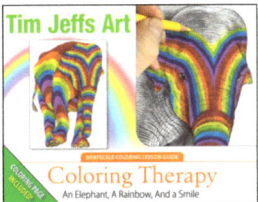 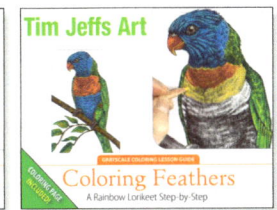

Available as print or instant download pdf books at:
TimJeffsArt.com • Etsy.com • Amazon.com

TIM JEFFS ART   Online Resources

Share Your Creativity with the World!

Join the ever-expanding coloring group of animal lovers who inspire each other through their colorings of the animals from Tim's books and lessons. With thousands of members from all around the world, Tim's Facebook group "Intricate Ink Coloring Group" is a creative and safe space where everyone is welcome. Jo Warren, the groups all-inspiring administrator will welcome you in with open arms and is there to encourage everyone to just have fun no matter your coloring skill level. Come join, we can't wait to have you as a member! Join Tim's Facebook Coloring Group at:

www.facebook.com/groups/intricateink

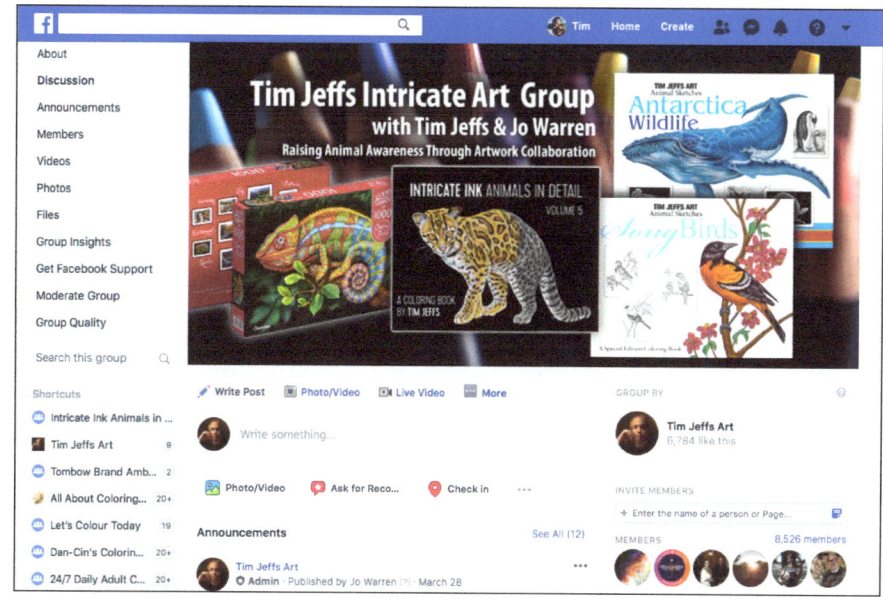

Visit the Home of Tim Jeffs Art

TimJeffsArt.com is my home on the web where I display all of my work and various projects. I hope you can stop by for a visit! You'll find my new shop where signed and unsigned prints of all of my animal drawings are available to purchase, along with the complete library of my digital download coloring books and grayscale coloring lessons. In the conservation section, you can see the projects that I am very proud of. Using my art to preserve wildlife is so important to me.

www.TimJeffsArt.com

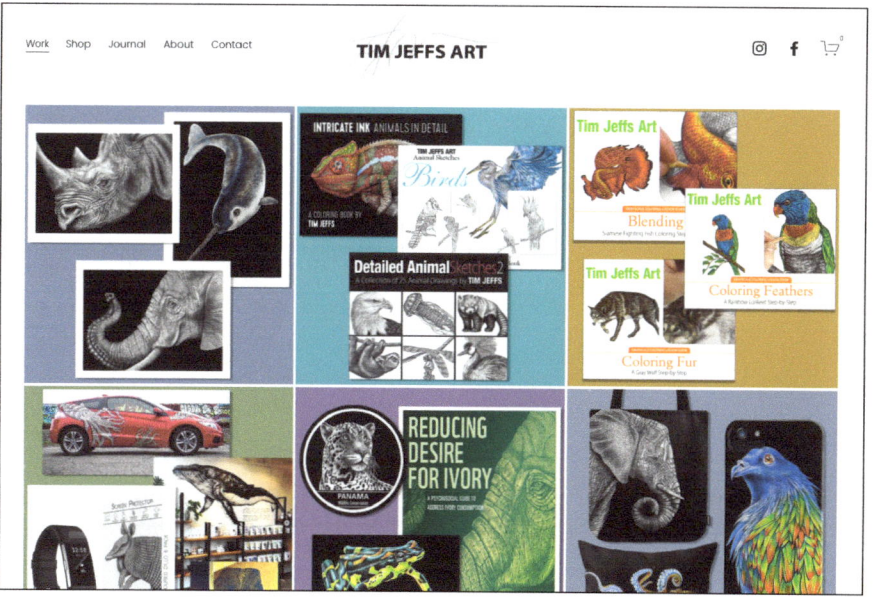